GOD PRINTS

Family funstuff
BIBLE STORIES
PRESCHOOL

Faith Kids™

Faith Kids® and Godprints™ are imprints of
Cook Communications Ministries, Colorado Springs, CO 80918
Cook Communications, Paris, Ontario
Kingsway Communications, Eastbourne, England

FAMILY FUNSTUFF BIBLE STORIES (PRESCHOOL)
©2001 by Cook Communications Ministries

First printing, 2001
Printed in Singapore

1 2 3 4 5 6 7 8 9 10 (printing/year) 05 04 03 02 01

Edited by: Lois Keffer and Susan Martins Miller

Written by: Marianne K. Hering, Lois Keffer, Janet Lee, Susan Martins Miller, Elizabeth Pippin, Gail Rohlfing, Jennifer Root Wilger

Cover and Interior Design: Helen Harrison at Ya Ye Design

Cover Illustration: Isidre Mones

Interior Illustration: Paige Billen-Frye, Stephen Carpenter, Shelly Dieterichs, Cary Pillo-Lassen, Jenny Williams, Vicki Woodworth

ISBN: 0-7814-3548-X

contents

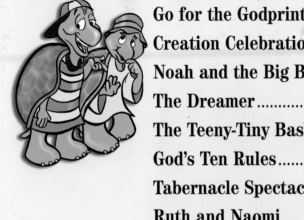

Go for the Godprint

The Bible was meant to be shared. By people of all ages for all time. By kids. By moms and dads and whole families.

The Bible is more than a collection of great stories—it's God's truth. For people of all ages for all time. For kids. For moms and dads and whole families. This treasury of Bible stories features a charming variety of interactive stories for little ones. Each turn of the page reveals something new and exciting.

The Bible was meant to be taken to heart and lived out. By kids. By moms and dads and whole families. So we've followed each Bible story with a Go for the Godprint section that helps kids and families do just that. In the Go for the Godprint pages you'll find:

The Godprint: What characteristic does God want to give kids that's illustrated in this story? This section presents the Godprint in language that's clear and challenging to preschoolers.

• **What's in Pouch's Pocket?:** Fun Bible tidbits that lead to a clearer understanding of the story.

• Two fun activities, crafts or games that help put feet on the Bible truth. It's great when kids learn Bible stories and think about them. It's better yet when kids live out what they've read! If your kids are learning from Godprints curriculum at church, they'll recognize the friendly characters from Potterfield Pond who host each activity.

- **Rocket's Rhymes:** Simple finger plays and songs for little fingers.

- **Nip & Tuck's Together Time:** Activities to explore the Godprint together.

- **Bumbles Hops to It:** Simple ways to serve others.

- **Mouse House Munchies:** Food fun to celebrate what God does for us.

- **Swoop's Art Cart:** Creative art and craft projects.

• **God Talk:** Creative, family-involving ways to pray.

Enjoy these pages of Bible adventure with your kids. And don't be surprised when Godprints start popping out all over your family!

Creation Celebration

Close your eyes and squeeze them tight. Tighter. As tight as you can.

Can you see anything? Imagine the world with no sun or stars, no trees, no animals, no people. Imagine the world with nothing in it at all. That's hard to do, isn't it?

In the very beginning, God decided to create our world. He started with a big ball of nothing at all.

The first thing God made was light. He said, "Let there be light." And there was light. With just four words, God made the first day.

On the second day, God said, "Let there be a great space." That big space is what we call the sky. When you look up at the sky, sometimes you see a big blue daytime sky. Sometimes you see a dark, quiet nighttime sky. God made the day and night.

Thank you, God, for making the day and night and the big sky over my head.

On the third day, the earth was covered with water. There was nowhere to walk or jump or climb. Just splishy, splashy water everywhere! So God pushed all the water into lakes, rivers and oceans. Then he made mountains, prairies, deserts and islands.

God liked what he had done, but he still had lots of work to do. He wanted his world to be colorful and fun for you. Can you guess what God created next? He made trees and flowers and fruits and vegetables. Yum!

On the fourth day God put lights in the sky. Guess what the lights were. A bright yellow sun to shine in the day and a silvery moon and stars to twinkle at night.

Thank you, God, for making plants and fruit and shiny stars.

When morning came on the fifth day, God looked out at his wonderful creation. He saw a big blue sky and a bright yellow sun. He saw pink and red and purple flowers. He saw mountains and valleys and oceans and streams.

God liked what he saw when he looked at his world, but he still wasn't finished. Do you know what he did next? God filled the waters with all kinds of animals that swim—fish and dolphins and whales. Then he filled the sky with birds. He made things that were alive!

Guess what God did on the sixth day of creation week. He made all the animals! Think about your favorite animal. Maybe it's furry or scaly. Maybe it's hairy or sleek. God made them all.

Thank you, God, for fish and birds and animals, especially my favorite one.

God's work was almost finished. There was only one thing left to make. Do you know what it was? People! God created man and woman. He made them so they could learn what's right and what's wrong and so they could love others, just as God does. The Bible tells us that God made people to be like him. That's why God loves us so much.

God took six days to make the world. He started with nothing. He finished by making people. On the seventh day, God took a rest!

God created a wonderful, amazing world for you and for me! So smell a flower, climb a tree, count the stars and eat ice cream. And remember to tell God "Thank you" for the world he made.

Thank you, God, for making me.

Awe and Wonder

When you hear the story of God's creation, aren't you amazed? God did such exciting things, don't you think? You can still find God's amazing work everywhere. His most awesome work is you! The Bible says that God made you in an amazing and wonderful way (Psalm 139:13–14). What other amazing things has God created that you can see today?

Bible Verse

God saw everything he had made. And it was very good.

Genesis 1:31

Swoop's Art Cart

Get List: charcoal briquette, pie tin, 6 tablespoons liquid laundry bluing, 6 tablespoons salt, 1 tablespoon ammonia, food coloring, mixing bowl and spoon.

Say, **God is amazing! He made our wonderful world out of nothing. The Bible says that in the beginning, the world was nothing. Then God made the sun, stars, animals and people.**

As a "creative" example make a little crystal garden starting with just a rock. Help your child break up the charcoal and place it in the pie tin. Mix all ingredients except the food coloring. Help your child pour the mixture carefully over the charcoal pieces. Sprinkle food coloring on the charcoal and place the pie tin in a safe, dry place. **Let's check on our garden every couple of hours and see what happens.** The garden should start to grow within six hours. As the garden crystals grow, talk with your child about the wonders of the garden and how much more wondrous is the work of God.

Mouse House Munchies

Get List: apple, cutting knife.

Say, **When God created the world, he filled it with wonderful things—giant crashing waterfalls, delicate white snowflakes, cuddly warm puppies and, of course, sweet little babies. God has also given us little treasures to find in his world**—white gleaming pearls inside of oyster shells, sweet thick honey inside of beehives and a treasure here inside this apple. Cut the apple in half crosswise rather than from top to bottom. Open the apple so your child can see the star shape inside. **What do you see? When we eat this apple or any apple from now on, we can think about God's wonderful creation and all the special things he has given us to enjoy on the earth.**

What's in Pouch's Pocket?

When God first created the world, rain did not fall from clouds to water the plants and fill the rivers. Guess where the water came from?

Streams of water rose up from the earth to moisten the ground (Genesis 2:5–6).

God Talk

Take a nature walk with your child and gather items of interest such as rocks, leaves or a piece of fallen fruit. When you return home, say a prayer of thanksgiving for each of the items that God created for our use and enjoyment.

Noah and the Big Boat

Noah was both kind and good.
He always did just what he should.
He loved the Lord with all his heart,
And trusted God right from the start.
　　For God was always with him.

But other people had turned bad,
And this made God feel very sad.
So God told Noah, "Build a boat.
I'll send a flood, but you will float."
　　For God was always with him.

Noah's saw and hammer flew
And day by day the great ark grew.
Screechy-screech! He sawed each plank.
His hammer went ta-tank, ta-tank.
    And God was always with him.

Then one fine day the boat was done.
But Noah's work had just begun.
God helped Noah start a zoo.
The creatures came on two by two.
    See? God was always with him!

Kangaroos and fuzzy hares
Hopped aboard in nice neat pairs.
Possums with their curling tails,
Birds and bugs and pokey snails.

Turtles, mice and fireflies,
Masked raccoons with big, bright eyes.
Zebras, hippos, elephants,
And baboons with their funny grunts.

Noah's family got on board.
God shut the door. Then thunder roared.
It rained for 40 days and nights
Until there was no land in sight.

Months went by—then, just like that
They bumped into Mount Ararat!
Noah thought it was just grand
When he could walk out on dry land.
    For God was always with him.

Noah built an altar there
And thanked God with a special prayer.
Then colors flashed across the sky
God made a rainbow. My, oh my!

God made this promise to his friend:
"I'll never send a flood again."
God's promises are always true,
True for Noah; true for you.
And God is always with us!

Go for the Godprint

Trust

We trust people who we know care about us. We can depend on them and believe what they say. People can sometimes let you down, but God won't. You can always trust God. He promised to take care of you, and God always keeps his promises.

Bible Verse

He is always there to help us in times of trouble.

Psalm 46:1

Nip & Tuck's Together Time

This game encourages preschoolers to imagine God in every place they will ever go. Pretend to be getting ready for a trip with your preschooler. You might use suitcases as props. Spread a blanket on the floor or set up chairs in a rectangle. Decide what type of transportation your blanket or chairs will be—a car, a plane, a rickshaw, a camel, a train or a bus.

Take your seats in the chairs or on the blanket. Act out all the things you normally would do to go on a trip. Once you start "traveling," talk with your child about where you are going, what you are seeing along the way, and what you will do when you get there. At the end of your "trip," remind your child that one reason we can trust God is because he is always with us.

Swoop's Art Cart

Get List: white coffee filters, watercolor paints, chenille wires, tape.

One of the reasons we can trust God is because he always keeps his promises. To remind your child of God's wonderful power, make a garden of promises by using watercolors to paint coffee filters. Talk about the rainbow colors your child is using to make the flowers. After the filters dry completely, use a permanent marker to write a different promise from God in the center of each flower. Some verses to start with are Psalm 27:5, Proverbs 18:10 and Philippians 4:19.

You may want to tape chenille wires to the back of your filter flowers as stems and make a bouquet for your table. Or tape the filters on mirrors throughout the house as reminders of the promises God has made.

What's in Pouch's Pocket?

It took Noah about 120 years to build the ark. Noah and his family took care of the animals in the ark for a little over a year. Part of the time they were floating, and part of the time they were waiting for the land to dry out.

God Talk

Gather the family together in the car for prayer. Your car represents all the places you go where God is with you. As you pray, name places your preschooler goes regularly and thank God for being with you there. End your prayer time by thanking God for being someone we can trust.

The Dreamer

Do you have brothers or sisters? Are you the youngest or oldest or are you somewhere in the middle?

This is a story about a boy with *eleven* older brothers. His name was Joseph and he lived in Canaan with his family. His father, Jacob, loved him best of all.

One day, Jacob gave Joseph a bright, colorful coat. Joseph wore it everywhere. When Joseph's brothers saw the coat, they got jealous. They wanted a coat like Joseph's.

Have you ever wanted something someone else had?
What did you do? Joseph's brothers got mad!

Joseph had another gift that made his brothers jealous. Joseph understood the hidden stories in dreams.

Do you ever dream? Do your dreams sometimes seem silly? Once Joseph dreamed he and his brothers were gathering wheat. Joseph's wheat stood up and the brothers' wheat bowed down. Another time, Joseph dreamed his father and mother were the sun and moon and his brothers were stars. In the dream, they bowed down to Joseph. Joseph told his brothers about his dreams and they got mad. They decided to get rid of Joseph. They sold him to some men from Egypt. Then they told their father a lie. They said Joseph had been eaten by a wild animal!

When Joseph got to Egypt, someone told a lie about him. He was sent to jail even though he didn't do anything wrong.

Maybe you've gotten in trouble for something you didn't do. What did you do? Well, Joseph just kept explaining dreams.

The king was having strange dreams. He dreamed about grain and cows. The king didn't understand any of his dreams. With God's help, Joseph explained the dreams to the king. He told the king the dreams meant there would be seven years of good crops and seven years when crops wouldn't grow. He told the king to save up lots of food so there would be enough when the bad years came.

The king was happy. Now he knew what his dream meant and he could make a plan. He put Joseph in charge of all the country's food. The time came when no food grew, but the people of Egypt had plenty to eat because Joseph had saved extra grain.

When Joseph's family ran out of food, some of the brothers went to Egypt to buy grain. They met Joseph, but they didn't recognize their brother they'd sent away so long ago.

They bowed down to him, and Joseph sold them food. Then the brothers went home.

When that food ran out, the brothers came back to buy more. They bowed down to Joseph again. It happened just as Joseph had dreamed long ago! This time Joseph told his brothers who he was. The brothers were scared. They thought Joseph would be mad at them. But he wasn't mad. Joseph forgave his brothers. He knew from his dreams that God had planned everything. Joseph had found the hidden story in his own dreams!

Each picture in this story has clues about Joseph. Can you look back and find the hidden story of Joseph's life?

19

Forgiveness

Saying "I'm sorry" can be one of the hardest things to do. But forgiving someone who hurts your feelings is harder still. God says we should forgive others just as he forgives us. He will help you forgive if you ask him. Do you know why God forgives you when you do wrong? Because he loves you!

Bible Verse

Forgive, just as the Lord forgave you.

Colossians 3:13

Nip & Tuck's Together Time

Get List: cassette tape and recorder, plain paper, markers, large zip-top bag, stapler.

Make your own family storybook about forgiveness by recording the story and drawing pictures to go with it. After you and your children record a story, listen to the tape, let your children draw pictures of what's happening and then make a book to go with the stories. Let each family member record a situation that requires forgiveness, such as borrowing something without asking, breaking a rule, or hurting someone's feelings. Add suggestions for ways to forgive in each situation. After recording the stories and creating the illustrations, staple the book together and store it with the tape in a zip-top bag. You can make other books on tape using themes such as prayer or friendship.

Swoop's Art Cart

Get List: cotton T-shirts for each family member, liquid fabric paint in several colors, pie tins, newspaper.

Have fun making colorful "Joseph's coat" T-shirts for your whole family! Cover a table with newspaper. Cover the bottom of each pie tin with a different paint color. Have each family member place an open hand in the paint, then make a palm print on a T-shirt. Repeat on all the T-shirts. Be sure to wash your hands when you change paint colors. Wear your "handiwork" as a reminder that God wants us to love and forgive each other just as he loves and forgives us.

What's in Pouch's Pocket?

Joseph was called "The Dreamer" because God talked to him in his dreams. Did you know God talked to Joseph's dad, Jacob, in his dreams too? (Genesis 28:12–15). Like father, like son!

God Talk

When someone really hurts your feeling or makes you sad, it can be hard to forgive them when they say "I'm sorry." Even when you make God sad, he will forgive you if you ask him. Next time you are angry because someone has done something wrong to you, say this little prayer:

God forgives me (clap, slap, clap).
I forgive you (clap, slap, clap).
Jesus loves me (clap, slap, clap).
And I love you (clap, slap, clap).

The Teeny-Tiny Basket Boat

"R-r-ribbit, r-r-ribbit," croaked the little frog. "Chirp. Chirp, chirp," answered the crickets. "Whish-swish, whish-swish," said the wind as it rushed through the tall grass. "Have you seen the teeny-tiny basket boat?" it seemed to say.

Basket boat? The Nile was a big, important river. People lived along its shores. Fish and frogs swam in its waters. What do you think a teeny-tiny basket boat was doing in the Nile River?

Plip-plippity-plop. The water gently splashed the basket boat as it floated down the river. Up and down, over the waves it went. The frogs and bugs hopped down the river's edge, hoping to see what was inside.

A little ways down the river, a girl watched the teeny-tiny basket boat. She smiled when she saw the boat bobbing up and down on the waves. The outside of the boat was covered with sticky tar to keep the water out. The boat was nice and dry inside.

Hippity-hop. R-r-ribbit, r-r-ribbit. The frogs followed the girl down the river bank. Splash-squelch. The grass squished beneath her feet.

Thump-bump. The teeny-tiny basket boat bumped over a rock in the river and turned to face the shore. A baby Hebrew boy was inside! The baby's mother had put him in the teeny-tiny basket boat to keep him safe from Pharaoh, the mean king of Egypt. He wanted to kill all the Hebrew baby boys because there were too many. The girl on the riverbank was the baby's sister, Miriam. She was watching to make sure the baby stayed safe and dry. As she watched, she sang a little song:

Rock-a-bye baby in your wee boat

That our momma made to keep you afloat.

God will take care of you now as you glide

Through the tall grasses that grow riverside.

Plip-plippity-plop. The teeny-tiny basket boat floated down the river and past Pharaoh's palace. Pharaoh's daughter was taking a bath in the river. She listened to the sounds of the river as she washed herself. She heard the frogs. R-r-ribbit, r-r-ribbit. She heard the crickets. Chirp. Chirp-chirp. She heard the wind whistling through the grass. Whish-swish, whish-swish. Then she heard a new sound. Waa! Waa!

The baby in the basket was crying! Pharaoh's daughter spotted the teeny-tiny basket boat and picked up the baby right away. Miriam asked her, "Would you like me to go and find someone to help you take care of the baby?"

"Yes, go," Pharaoh's daughter said. Right away, Miriam ran home and brought back her own mother. Miriam and her mother took care of the baby until he was old enough to live with Pharaoh's daughter. They named the baby Moses, and he grew up to be a great leader for God's people.

God's Ten Rules

Get the tents up. Start the fire. Look for some water. It's time to set up camp.

God's people camped near a mountain. They were in a big desert. Imagine their surprise when one day the whole mountain shook! A thick dark cloud of smoke covered the mountain. Thunder and lightning cracked open the sky. Crash! A loud trumpet sound blasted through the air, louder and louder and louder.

God came to the mountain that day. He had a message for his people.

God called Moses, the leader of the people, to the top of the mountain. So Moses climbed into the cloud with its lightning and thunder. The people waited at the bottom of the mountain to find out what God's message was.

God gave Moses 10 rules for the people to follow. God gave these rules because he loved his people and wanted them know the best way to live. These rules are called the Ten Commandments.

Some of the Ten Commandments helped the people love God better. The first commandment God gave Moses was the most important one: love God more than anyone or anything else. That showed God how much the people loved him.

Another commandment was for the people to work for six days each week. On the next day, the seventh day, the people should rest and worship God.

Some of the commandments helped the people get along with each other. One of God's commandments was special for children. God wants children to love and obey their parents.

God said, "Do not kill anyone. Do not steal." That means do not take anything that doesn't belong to you. God said, "Do not lie or say bad things about another person." God said, "Do not want something that belongs to someone else."

God wrote these 10 rules on two stone tablets with his own finger. Imagine that!

When Moses went back down the mountain, he told all the people about God's Ten Commandments.

God's Ten Commandments are written in the Bible. They are God's rules for us too. God wants us to obey his rules to show we love him.

Obedience

What do you feel like when you obey your mom and dad the very first time they ask you to pick up your toys? Obeying because you want to is so much better than obeying because you have to. God's Ten Commandments are for us to follow too. Sometimes it might be hard to obey these rules. But God helps us obey because we want to, not because we have to.

Bible Verse

I will obey your word.
Psalm 119:17

Nip & Tuck's Together Time

God gives us rules to obey. Play a game of "Simon Says" to reinforce the idea of following rules.

Choose a family member to be Simon. "Simon" should tell the rest of the family to do certain actions, such as rub your tummy. Some of the actions need to have the phrase "Simon says..." in the beginning. These are the only actions family members should do. If a person does an action that doesn't begin with "Simon says," that person doesn't play for a turn. Play several times with different family members playing the part of Simon. After you play, talk about:

• Why did we have to follow what "Simon" said?

• What happened when we didn't obey "Simon"?

• How is following the rules of the game like following God's rules?

Mouse House Munchies

Get List: 1 package refrigerator biscuits, canned apple pie filling, 1/2 cup sifted powdered sugar, 1 teaspoon butter or margarine, 1 tablespoon milk.

Use this simple recipe for apple tarts to talk about obeying God.

Press the biscuits on a cookie sheet until they are 1/4 inch thick.

Spread two to three tablespoons of pie filling on each biscuit. Bake at 350 degrees for 10 to 12 minutes. Cool.

To make the frosting, melt the butter. Pour the butter into the powdered sugar. Stir, adding enough milk to make a thin frosting. Frost the tarts. While you enjoy your snack, talk about:

- What would happen if we didn't follow the directions to make our tarts?
- What if we put the biscuits on top of the apples?
- Why should we obey God's Commandments?

What's in Pouch's Pocket?

God's Ten Commandments are part of a promise between God and his people. God wrote the promise on two big pieces of stone.

God Talk

Find a small smooth stone for each member of the family. Hold them in your hands while you pray together about following God's rules. When prayer time is over, have everyone put a stone in the pocket of clothing or a jacket. Touching the stone will be a reminder of the rules God wrote in stone on the mountain.

Tabernacle Spectacular

As you read this story, ask your child to repeat each line back to you. For added fun, clap your hands or slap your knees as you say each line.

Let's build a tabernacle.
Gonna worship God there.
Every house and family
Needs to do its share.

Let's build a tabernacle.
Come on, bring your gold.
Bring your bronze, your silver, too—
There's room for young and old.

Let's build a tabernacle.
We'll need a lot of stuff.
Like scarlet yarn and onyx stones—
I hope we'll have enough.

Let's build a tabernacle.
Gonna worship God there.
Every house and family
Needs to do its share.

Let's build a tabernacle.
Here's purple yarn and blue.
Acacia wood and red ram skins
And olive oil, too.

Let's build a tabernacle.
We'll follow God's command.
Then God will come and guide us
As we travel through this land.

Let's build a tabernacle.
Gonna worship God there.
Every house and family
Needs to do its share.

Let's build a tabernacle.
It's looking pretty nice.
All we need to finish up
Are incense, gems and spice.

Let's build a tabernacle.
Our work is nearly past.
With help from each and every house
We'll soon be done—at last!

36

Let's build a tabernacle.
Gonna worship God there.
Every house and family
Needs to do its share.

Let's build a tabernacle.
Our gifts we gladly bring.
We lay them at the altar
As we worship God our King.

We built a tabernacle.
And everyone helped out.
We shared our things and shared the work.
That's what it's all about.

Ruth and Naomi

Use different voices for each character as you read this drama.

Once long, long ago, God's people in Israel were hungry. It hadn't rained for a long time, so the crops didn't grow. One man took his family to live in the faraway land of Moab where there was more food. The family's two sons grew up and got married. After many years, the man died. Then the sons died too. That left just the mother, Naomi, and her son's wives, Orpah and Ruth. Poor Naomi! She missed her husband and sons. She decided it would be best to go back to live in her hometown of Bethlehem.

NAOMI (worriedly): Oh, what will I do now! I have no one to care for me and I am far from my homeland. Orpah, Ruth, my dears, it is time for me to leave you and go back to Bethlehem.

ORPAH (sadly): Then I will also go back to my family so I have someone to care for me. I will be sorry to see you go.

RUTH (strongly): I can never leave you, Naomi. You are like a mother to me. Wherever you go, I will go. Let me make my home with you. And I will worship your God as you do.

NAOMI (gratefully): I will be happy to have you with me. Let's go back to my homeland.

So Ruth and Naomi traveled to Bethlehem. Things were different than when Naomi left so many years before. Now there were good crops and plenty to eat.

RUTH: Naomi, we are almost out of grain for bread. Let me go into the grain fields and gather grain after the workers.

NAOMI: Thank you, Ruth. That is a good idea.

Ruth went to a field to pick up pieces of grain left behind by the harvesters. She did not know it, but the field belonged to a kind friend of Naomi's family. His name was Boaz. He came to the field to see how the harvest was going.

BOAZ (cheerfully): Hello, everyone! May God be good to you. Who is that young woman gathering grain?

MAN: Her name is Ruth. She came back with Naomi. She has been working hard all day.

BOAZ: Ruth, you are welcome to stay in my field. You will be safe here. You will get lots of grain, and if you are thirsty, you can help yourself to my water.

RUTH: Why are you being so kind to me? I am a stranger here.

BOAZ: You may not know me, but I know about you. I have heard how you have taken care of Naomi. Now I want to be kind to you.

Boaz found many ways to be kind to Ruth. He took care of her and made sure she was safe. He had the workers leave extra grain for her to gather. That way Ruth gathered enough grain to take good care of Naomi.

One happy day Ruth and Boaz got married! Before long, they had a baby boy named Obed. Grandma Naomi was so happy to have a baby in the house again! She helped take good care of little Obed.

Obed's great-grandson was King David. From King David's family, Jesus was born!

God helped Ruth care for Naomi. God helped Boaz care for Ruth. God helps us care for each other.

Go for the Godprint

Kindness

Kindness is doing something nice for someone—just because. When you help pick up without being asked, that is being kind. When you give a hug to someone who is sad, that is being kind. Our words can show kindness too. Saying "please" and "thank you" and "I'm sorry" or "I love you" are ways we can show we care about others.

Bible Verse

Be kind...to one another.
Ephesians 4:32

Swoop's Art Cart

Get List: poster board, markers, ribbons, stickers and other craft supplies.

Invite your child to help make a chart of specific ways to care for others during the next week. Decorate your chart with colorful lettering, pictures and bright ribbons. Draw fun shapes large enough to print a caring action inside. Some caring actions might be giving a hug, using kind words (like please and thank you), helping with a chore or sharing. Write the memory verse across the bottom of your art chart.

Post your art chart in a central location in your home. Use stickers or smiley faces to celebrate each time your child shows care for others in one of the ways shown. Have a special place to celebrate new acts of kindness not listed on the chart.

Mouse House Munchies

Get List: pita bread, and some of the following items for filling—peanut butter and jelly, meat and cheese, veggies, chicken salad.

Make a pocket-bread sandwich snack to share. Explain that the flat bread you are using is similar to the type of bread Ruth and Naomi would have made.

As you assemble and eat your snack, talk about specific ways you care for your child, for others in your family and for neighbors and friends. Encourage your child to talk about ways he or she can care for others.

What's in Pouch's Pocket?

The grain that Ruth gathered was probably barley or wheat. The field was just outside of Bethlehem where Jesus was born. In Bible times letting poor people gather leftover grain was one way to help them.

God Talk

Gather photos of friends and family. Talk with your child about how God has helped each person pictured to care for others. Place the photos in a circle on the floor with you and your child standing in the center. Close your eyes and spin around. Open your eyes and pick up the photo nearest to you. Stop and pray with your child, thanking God for the person in the photo and asking God to help us to care for others. Next time, let your child spin.

45

from 1 Samuel 1-3

Samuel and the Mysterious Voice

Once there was a woman named Hannah. She wanted a baby very much. She waited and waited for a baby.

Are you three years old? Hannah waited longer than that.

Are you four years old? Hannah waited longer than that.

Are you five years old? Hannah waited longer than that. That's a very long time to wait. But no baby came.

Hannah went to the Lord's house with her husband and prayed to God for a baby. Hannah promised that if God would give her a baby, she would give the baby back to God to work for him.

A priest named Eli heard Hannah pray and ask God for a baby. Eli told Hannah to go home. He told Hannah that God would give her what she asked for.

At home, Hannah waited. Guess what? God *did* hear Hannah's prayer. God gave her a baby boy! Hannah named her baby Samuel. She kept the promise she made to God.

When Samuel was old enough for the priests to take care of him, Hannah took him to the Lord's house. Now Samuel could learn how to serve God.

One night, Samuel woke up. He heard someone calling his name. He thought it was Eli, so he went to Eli's room. But it wasn't Eli who had called him.

Samuel went back to bed. Someone called him again. He went back to Eli again, but it still wasn't Eli who had called him.

Then someone called him again! Who do you think might be calling Samuel? Eli knew. It was God calling Samuel. Eli told Samuel to say, "Yes, Lord, I am listening" when he heard the voice again.

Samuel was lying in his bed. He heard the voice call his name again. Samuel knew it wasn't Eli. He knew that God was talking to him. "Yes, Lord, I am listening," Samuel said, just like Eli had told him.

God started talking to Samuel. He told Samuel things that the people needed to know. When Samuel grew up, he told God's message to the people. God used Samuel to teach the people the things God wanted them to know. Samuel was God's prophet.

from
1 Samuel
17:1-24,
31-50

Boy Versus Giant

When you read the name "Goliath*," you and your child can slap your legs three times, like the steps of a giant. When you read the name "David*," put your fists in the air and say "HOO-rah!" The names are marked with an asterisk (*) to remind you to pause.

Imagine the biggest, meanest bully ever. That was Goliath*—the hero of the Philistines.

The Philistines were enemies of God's people. The Philistines wanted Goliath* to fight one of Israel's soldiers. But the Israelites didn't have anyone as big as the giant Goliath*.

In his bare feet, Goliath* stood nine feet four inches tall—as tall as a grizzly bear! He wore a heavy armor all over his body. How could anyone fight him and win?

Every day Goliath went out on the hillside and made fun of the Israelite soldiers.

"I'm big and I'm tough. See me? I'm the champ.
No one can beat me from the Israelite camp.
Where is your hero? Are you all wimps?
Who will come fight me? You're scared little shrimps."

The Israelites were scared of him. Not even their king wanted to fight the giant.

One day a boy named David* came to camp to bring food to his brothers. When he heard Goliath's* mean talk, David* went to King Saul.

"What that giant is saying just isn't right.
Give me a chance at him. I'll go and fight."

King Saul wanted David* to use his royal clothes and armor. But everything was too big. So David* went out to face Goliath* with only a sling and five stones. In his bare feet, David* stood only as tall as a grizzly cub. But his faith in God was bigger than 10 giants.

When Goliath* saw who was coming, he laughed.

"You're sending a boy? This must be a joke.
I'll finish this fight with one little poke."

54

David* put a stone in his sling. He whirled it and whirled it and then let it go. SWOOSH! The stone flew through the air. WHOMP! It hit the giant's head. SMACK! Goliath* fell into the dirt. And that was the end of the giant.

When a boy beats a giant, some folks think it's odd.
But I know it's 'cuz of our wonderful God.
God is the strongest—he's always the champ
He helped David save the whole Israelite camp.

David's Best Buddy

David was a shepherd. He lived in a little house in the fields.

Jonathan was a prince, the son of King Saul. He lived in the palace.

After David killed Goliath, David and Jonathan became friends. Even though their lives were different, they loved each other.

Can you point to David? Can you point to Jonathan? Do you have a good friend?

Jonathan liked to share his things with David. Can you name the things that Jonathan gave to David?

Jonathan shared his robe, belt, sword and bow with David. Then David and Jonathan promised they would always be friends.

Jonathan was a good friend to David. But Jonathan's father, King Saul, didn't like David. Saul was jealous because David had killed Goliath. Saul thought that the people liked David better than they liked him.

Jonathan told David, "Be very careful. My father is angry with you. He might try to hurt you."

It was a hard time for David and Jonathan. Jonathan loved his father, but he couldn't let King Saul hurt his best friend. Jonathan promised to help David get away from King Saul.

How do you and your friends help each other in hard times?

Jonathan and David agreed on a special signal. Jonathan brought out his bow and arrow. If King Saul was still trying to hurt David, Jonathan would shoot the arrows behind his servant boy. If it was safe for David to come back to King Saul's palace, Jonathan would shoot the arrows in front of his servant boy.

One day David hid behind a big rock. He watched carefully for Jonathan's arrows. When David heard Jonathan tell his servant, "Aren't the arrows behind you?" he knew that it wasn't safe for him to stay near the palace.

David was sad to leave his best friend, Jonathan. Both of them cried. They promised to help each other forever. And that's what they did.

Friendliness

Jonathan showed his love for David by helping him get away from King Saul. He could have told David, "Sorry, I can't help you." But instead he did what David needed. Loving a friend means thinking about what your friend needs instead of thinking only of selfish things. So the next time a friend comes to play, try asking, "What would you like to do?"

Bible Verse

Friends love at all times.
Proverbs 17:17

Swoop's Art Cart

Get List: large sheet of construction paper, washable paints or a washable inkpad, clear adhesive paper, wet paper towels.

Have "friends for dinner" permanently by making these simple place mats. Help each friend or family member make thumbprints on sheets of construction paper. Continue stamping until everyone's thumbprint is on each person's paper. Have fun making designs with the thumbprints! Keep wet paper towels on hand for easy cleanup.

After the thumbprints are dry, write the words "Friends for Dinner" on each place mat, then cover the place mats with clear adhesive paper. Use the place mats as a mealtime reminder to thank God for the friends he's given you.

Bumbles Hops to it

Invite another preschooler to your home for a play date. Before your friend arrives, talk with your child about sharing, using kind words and other behaviors that foster friendships. As the children play together, praise positive friendship behaviors as they occur. Afterward talk with your child about the things he or she did to be a good friend to your guest. Remind your child that a friend loves at all times.

What's in Pouch's Pocket?

Because Jonathan was a prince, David was invited to eat dinner at the royal palace. They probably had roast meat such as lamb or venison. A common fruit to eat was the pomegranate. Most meals had some sort of bread too.

God Talk

Help your child pray for a different preschool friend each morning before school. (If your child doesn't attend preschool, choose friends from Sunday school.) Talk with your child about what makes each friend unique and special, then help him or her pray: "Thank you, God, for Ryan. I'm glad he's my friend."

Thrown to the Lions

from Daniel 6

I am King Darius, mighty king of Babylon. I rule over all the people, and they bow down to me. I get to say what the laws are, and anyone who breaks the laws is punished.

But I am also a good man. I am fair and take care of the Babylonian people. I listen to the advice of the men who work for me. One of my favorite advisers is Daniel. He always seems to have the right answers for everything. Daniel loves God and prays to him every-day. I didn't used to care about God. I thought everyone should worship me instead. After all, I'm the king!

64

Some of the men who work for me don't like Daniel because he is smart and kind. I think they are jealous because I always listen to Daniel. They know that, even though Daniel and I are good friends, Daniel loves God best of all. They also know that I would never want anything bad to happen to Daniel. These men are mean and sneaky. They talked me into making a law that said people could only worship me and no one else. They knew that Daniel would still pray to God.

One day they spied on him and caught him worshiping God. They threw him in jail because he broke my law. Now I would have to punish Daniel. After all, I am the king!

The mean, sneaky men brought Daniel to me. They wanted to throw him into the lions' den! That would be the end of Daniel. Those hungry lions would eat him up in no time.

I was so sad. Daniel was my friend. I didn't want anything to happen to him. But I was the mighty king of Babylon. If I didn't punish Daniel for breaking my law, people would think I was weak. Maybe they wouldn't bow down before me. Maybe they would get rid of me!

I ordered Daniel into the lions' den. "May your God save you!" I said to my friend. Then I told the soldiers to seal the door to the lions' den. After all, I am the king!

Even though I am Darius, the mighty king of Babylon, I didn't sleep at all that night. I was so worried about my friend Daniel. I was angry too. I knew those men had tricked me into making that law so Daniel would get in trouble. Daniel would never trick me like that.

Finally, it was morning. I jumped out of bed and ran all the way to the lions' den. I yelled through the door, "Daniel, Daniel! Did your God save you?" Then I heard the most wonderful sound. It was Daniel's voice!

"Yes, King Darius," he said. "God sent an angel to shut the lions' mouths." I knew then that Daniel was right all along. I made a new law that all the people in Babylon should worship God. After all, I am the king!

Jonah's Undersea Adventure

Show your child each of the four pictures in the rebus key and read the words they replace. Your child can "read" along with you by saying the rebus word when you get to each picture.

KEY:

Jonah

Nineveh

Boat

Giant Fish

God had a message for . "Go to  and tell the people about me. Tell them I want them to stop doing bad things." But  didn't like the people in . He decided not to obey God. In fact, he got on a  that was going in the opposite direction!

Where was ?  was trying to run away from God.

The  was on the sea when a wild storm came up. The wind and the waves tossed the  so badly that the sailors thought it would break into pieces. They prayed to their gods and threw things overboard, but still they thought the  would sink. Everyone on the  was doomed!

Where was ?  was fast asleep below the deck.

When the captain of the  woke up, realized right away that God was trying to get his attention. He knew he should have followed God's plan and gone to . He told the men on the everything and said, "Throw me overboard. This is all my fault. I didn't obey God. Throw me in the sea and the storm will stop."

The men on the didn't want to throw overboard. But it was the only thing left to do. As soon as hit the water, the storm stopped. The men on the board knew then that God controlled the wind and the waves and they worshiped him.

Where was ? was drowning in the sea.

But God had not given up on  . God sent a  to save  .
The  was so big it swallowed  without taking a bite!

Where was  ?  was safe in the belly of the  .

 was inside the  for three days and three nights. What do you
think  did inside that  ?  talked to God. He told God how
afraid he had been in the stormy sea. He thanked God for saving him from
the deep waters. He praised God for sending the  to keep him safe.
And he promised God he would obey and go to  .

God heard all that  said inside the 's belly. God told the to spit out onto dry land. And the obeyed God and did just what he said.

Where was ? was back on dry land.

God told again to go to , and this time obeyed. He told all the people in the big city of about God. The people of were sorry. They wanted to change. God helped obey him. God helped the people of obey him. God helps us obey him too.

Go for the Godprint

Submissiveness

It's hard to do something you don't want to do—like when your parents ask you to put away your toys while you still want to play. But by obeying and doing it right away you show love to the one who asked you. God sometimes asks us to do something that is hard—something we don't really want to do. God knows what is best for us, so he helps us obey.

Bible Verse

Do what is right and good in the LORD's eyes.
Deuteronomy 6:18

Nip & Tuck's Together Time

Playing a variation of the game "Mother, May I?" will help your child practice submissiveness in real ways. Have your preschooler stand across the room from you. Explain that you will give your child an action to act out. But first your child must ask permission by saying "Mother (or Father), may I?" If you respond "Yes, you may," your child can do the action. But if you say, "No, you may not," your child must wait for the next action you name.

Start by suggesting actions such as hop up and down, clap your hands or take three steps forward. Next move into suggestions that reflect actions you want to teach your child about such as, pick up your toys, make a happy face or give a hug. Use this game to teach and to reinforce instructions you expect your child to obey.

74

Mouse House Munchies

Get List: 1 package blue gelatin mix, 4 to 6 candy fish, 4 to 6 clear plastic glasses, whipped cream topping.

By making this tasty snack with your child, you have a chance to "fish" for answers to questions about the story. Make the gelatin according to the directions on the package. Pour the gelatin into the clear plastic glasses. Place a candy fish in the middle of the gelatin in each glass. Refrigerate until the gelatin is set. Top with whipped cream "waves" before eating. Now you have an edible giant fish in the sea. As you enjoy your snack with your preschooler, talk about these questions:

• Where's Jonah? (He's inside the fish, of course!)
• What's he doing? (Talking to God.)
• What do you think he is saying to God? (Thank you for helping me obey.)

What's in Pouch's Pocket?

Nineveh was a very large and important city. Each of its five walls were so wide that you could ride around its top with four chariots and horses running shoulder to shoulder.

God Talk

Try to recall specific times when your child has shown submissiveness recently. Use the following prayer as a guide to pray a personal prayer of encouragement for your child:

Dear God, sometimes it is hard to obey. But you have promised to help us obey. Thank you for the time (your child's name and an example of how submissiveness was demonstrated). We want to do what is good and right in your eyes. In Jesus' name, amen.

Joy, Joy, Joy!

Hello there. I'm Manger Mouse. They call me Manger Mouse because I live in this manger. The cows and sheep keep their food in here, and they're usually kind enough to leave me a small morsel. But as you can see, tonight I've given my home to someone a little more important.

Joy, joy, joy! A baby boy is in my manger. He was born here last night. His parents, Mary and Joseph, must have had a long journey. They were sure tired when they got here. I hear they're counting people in our town, so they must have come to be counted.

A baby boy sleeping in my manger—Field Mouse is not going to believe this. I've gotta tell him!

Joy, joy, joy! I'm Field Mouse, and I just heard that a baby boy is sleeping in Manger Mouse's manger. I'm on my way over to see the little fellow, but first I've gotta find out what that bright light is out in the field. I hope it doesn't scare the sheep, or there'll be a stampede.

Look up in the sky! That's no ordinary starlight. No, something exciting is about to happen. Joy, joy, joy! I overheard a shepherd say the light was coming from an angel!

"Do not be afraid," the angel said. "I bring you good news of great joy that will be for all the people. Today in the town of David a Savior has been born to you; he is Christ, the Lord. This will be a sign to you: You will find a baby wrapped in cloths and lying in a manger."

In a manger! Well, joy, joy, joy! I must hurry and tell Manger Mouse.

Finally when everyone was sure that the boat would sink, we woke Jesus up.

We told him that the storm was going to sink the boat and everyone would die. Jesus sat up and looked at all of us. We were so afraid. Some of us were shaking and crying. But Jesus didn't shake. He didn't cry. He asked us calmly, "Why are you so afraid? Where is your trust in God?"

Why *were* we afraid? We had Jesus with us the whole time!

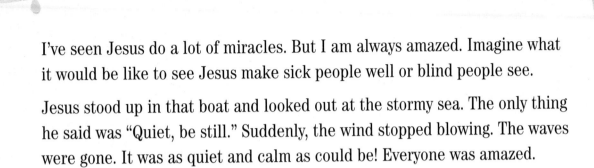

I've seen Jesus do a lot of miracles. But I am always amazed. Imagine what it would be like to see Jesus make sick people well or blind people see.

Jesus stood up in that boat and looked out at the stormy sea. The only thing he said was "Quiet, be still." Suddenly, the wind stopped blowing. The waves were gone. It was as quiet and calm as could be! Everyone was amazed. Who was this man who could tell the wind and the sea what to do? I knew. It was Jesus.

The Man Who Couldn't Walk

I can't move my legs. I can't walk or run or jump. I can't even wiggle my toes.

But I have good friends who help me. When I need to go somewhere, they put me on a mat. Each friend takes a corner of the mat and lifts. They carry me wherever I need to go. One friend couldn't pick me up all by himself, but all together my friends can help me. I may not have good legs, but I have good friends.

But I still would like to stand up and walk. I've heard about a man named Jesus. Crowds of people listen to him teach. My friends say he even heals sick people. I wonder if Jesus can heal me so I can walk.

I heard that Jesus is in our town today. He is teaching at a nearby house. My friends are going to carry me to see Jesus!

When we arrive at the house, it's jam-packed with people. They want to hear what Jesus has to say. So many people have come that we can't get inside the house to see Jesus. We can't even get close to the door. But we know Jesus is there. We can hear him talking.

My friends don't give up. They think of a way for me to see Jesus.

This house is like many buildings in our town. It has stairs on the outside. The stairs go up to the roof. My friends pick up my mat and carry me up to the top of the house. Then they dig through the roof until there's a hole big enough for my mat. Usually my friends lift me up. Now they're lowering me down—right through the hole in the roof. There is Jesus!

The people in the house are surprised to see me. Now I am right in front of Jesus. He knows that my friends and I believe he can fix my legs. He knows it took a lot of work for my friends to get me there. Jesus is proud of me and my friends. Not everybody would think to make a hole in the roof to see him. So what do you think Jesus does when he sees me?

He says "Get up. You can take your mat and go home."

I get up. My legs are working! Jesus healed me! I roll up my mat and walk. Yippee! I praise God for the wonderful things Jesus does—and for my good friends too.

Creativity

In the Bible story, the man and his friends knew Jesus could help the man walk. When the crowd blocked their way to Jesus, the man and his friends used their imaginations to find a way to solve the problem. God gives us special gifts to solve problems too. We can use these gifts when we play, color, sing and tell God that we love him. That's creativity!

Bible Verse

Everyone was amazed and gave praise to God.

Luke 5: 26

Swoop's Art Cart

Get List: large pieces of paper or cardboard, two colors of washable tempera paints, paint shirts, clean items found around the house such as flyswatters, forks, old toothbrushes or sponges to use as paint brushes.

This activity allows each family member to use creativity to create a Praise Picture. Give each family member a large piece of paper. Use the different "brushes" and paints to create a picture. Each picture will be unique. Encourage different blends of colors and patterns with the brushes. When the paintings are dry, display them in a "Gifts of God" art gallery. Spend time looking at each person's picture. Point out something unique in each painting to emphasize the different gifts and creativity in your family.

Rocket's Rhymes

Teach the following finger play to your child to review the Bible story.

Here is a man who cannot walk. *(Hold up your index finger.)*

He lies upon a mat. *(Lay your right finger on your left palm.)*

Here are the friends *(Hold up four fingers.)*

Who picked up the mat *(Lay your right index finger on your left palm.)*

And took him to Jesus one day.

The house was so full *(Fold hands with fingers laced on top.)*

They opened the roof *(Unlace hands and hold them open.)*

And lowered the mat in that way. *(Lay your right finger on your left palm. Bring your palm down.)*

What's in Pouch's Pocket?

Many houses in Bible times had a flat roof and a staircase on the outside of the house. Some people used the roof as another room.

God Talk

Work together to build a house out of blocks or another kind of building toy. Try to make a roof covering the house. In the Bible story the man and his friends found a way to see Jesus. They were creative. God has given each of us special ways to be creative. Take turns thanking God for gifts of imagination and insight. As each person finishes, he or she can take off part of the roof.

93

Jesus and Jairus

Wherever Jesus went, lots and lots of people followed him. They wanted to hear him tell stories. They hoped he would make the sick people well. They knew he was kind and good. (Can you find Jesus in the picture?)

Jairus was an important man in the synagogue. (Can you find Jairus?) The synagogue was like a church—a place where people could learn about God. Jairus had a little girl who was 12 years old. He loved her with his whole heart. But she was sick, and Jairus was afraid she would die. Jairus didn't know what to do. So he went to Jesus.

While Jesus was talking, Jairus suddenly stepped from the crowd. "Jesus!" he cried. When Jesus turned to see who had called his name, Jairus fell at Jesus' feet. "Jesus, please! My little girl is very sick. I know you can make her well. Please come!"

Jesus was on his way. He was going with Jairus to help his sick little girl. But then someone came from Jairus's house with a sad message: Jairus's daughter was dead.

When Jesus heard this, he felt sad for Jairus. "Don't worry, Jairus," Jesus said kindly. "You came to me because you believed I could help your little girl. Just keep believing in me, and she will still get well."

Soon they arrived at Jairus's house. What a noise greeted them! People were crying and wailing, moaning and groaning. "Stop your loud crying," Jesus told them. "This little girl is not dead. She is sleeping."

The people laughed at Jesus. "What is wrong with him?" they thought. They could tell the little girl was dead. But Jesus passed right by them. Only the little girl's parents and three of Jesus' friends went into the little girl's room with him.

Jesus knew how precious that little girl was to her mommy and her daddy. She was precious to Jesus too. So he gently took her hand and said, "Little girl, get up!"

Right away, the little girl opened her eyes and jumped out of bed. "She's hungry," Jesus told them. "Give her something to eat." Jairus and his family could hardly believe what had happened! Their precious little girl was alive and well. Jesus had shown them that God cares when we're hurt.

The Good Friend

Adding simple sound effects (marked in parentheses) as you tell this Bible story favorite will make it more fun for your preschooler. Encourage your child to help you make the noises.

Jesus told a story about a traveler, some robbers and three men. Only one of the men was a true friend to the traveler. Listen to find out which man was the friend.

(Clap cupped hands together to make the sound of a donkey walking.) A traveler was riding his donkey along the dusty road to the city of Jericho. Whomp! Suddenly he was attacked by a bunch of wild robbers. The men pulled him off his donkey, beat him up and took all his money. Then the robbers rode off with his donkey and left the man to die. *(Clap cupped hands quickly.)*

"Oh," moaned the man, "please, can someone help me? I am too hurt to move. I need a friend to help me." But no one could hear him. He put his head down in the dirt and waited to die.

A while later a priest came walking down the road. *(Stomp feet slowly.)* "What is that lump at the side of the road up ahead?" wondered the man. *(Whisper.)* "I must be careful. This is a dangerous road. It could be a trick." He put his head down and kept walking straight ahead. As the priest got closer, he noticed that the lump was moving just a little. It was the hurt traveler.

"Oh," moaned the man, "please, can someone help me? I am too hurt to move. I need a friend to help me." But the priest put his hands over his ears so he wouldn't have to hear the moaning. He quickly walked to the other side of the road and was soon out of sight. *(Stomp feet quickly.)*

A while later a lawyer came walking down the road. *(Stomp feet quickly.)* He was humming *(hum)* and thinking as he hurried along, "I have so much to do when I get to Jericho. I must read the law and talk with the other lawyers." As he walked nearer to the hurt man, he stopped humming to listen. "I think that lump in the road is making a noise," he thought.

"Oh," moaned the man, "please, can someone help me? I am too hurt to move. I need a friend to help me." But the lawyer was too busy to help a poor man. He started humming louder and walking faster along the other side of the road and was soon out of sight. *(Stomp feet and hum rapidly.)*

A while later a Samaritan man came riding his donkey down the road. *(Clap cupped hands together.)* No one really liked the Samaritans very much. No one thought anyone from Samaria could be a good friend. But when the Samaritan saw the hurt traveler by the road, he didn't cover his hears, he didn't hum on by. Instead he jumped off his donkey and ran to see if he could help. *(Run feet in place.)*

"Oh, you poor man! You have been hurt badly. I will be a friend and help you," said the Samaritan. He washed the man's cuts and put bandages on them. He placed him on his own donkey. Carefully the Samaritan took the hurt traveler *(clap cupped hands slowly)* to a nearby inn and used his own money to pay for someone to take care of the man until he was well. When he was sure the traveler would be all right, he continued on his own journey.

After Jesus told this story he asked, "Which man was a good friend to the traveler?" The Samaritan was a good friend because he helped the hurt man. God wants friends to help each other.

Friendliness

Think about someone you like to play with and who makes you smile. It's good to have friends—someone who likes you for being you, who will share with you and who is fun to be with. But it is even better to be a friend. God wants us to be friends with other people.

Bible Verse

Give to the one who asks you for something.

Matthew 5:42

Swoop's Art Cart

Make craft dough from 1 cup salt, 2 cups flour and 1 scant cup water. Let your child help you knead the dough. Then roll it and cut out "people" with gingerbread cookie cutters. Allow the craft-dough people to air-dry until they're hard (or speed up the process by putting them in the oven on a low temperature setting for about one hour). Use markers to decorate the figures together to create "friends" who look like your real-life friends. As you work together, talk about how God wants friends to help each other. Discuss ways your preschooler could help a friend.

Bumbles Hops to it

Have a "friendship" brainstorming time with your preschooler and others in your family. You may want to use a piece of poster board and write down ways to complete the sentence "A friend is someone who...." Write down everyone's responses. Look up Bible verses that talk about friends, such as Proverbs 17:17, Ecclesiastes 4:10, Luke 6:31 or John 13:34. Then ask everyone in the family to choose one way to work on being a friend to others during the coming week. Set a time to check in with everyone later to see how things are going.

What's in Pouch's Pocket?

The road from Jerusalem to Jericho was steep and rocky. It had lots of good places for robbers to hide.

God Talk

Buy an inexpensive box of plain bandages. When your child shares a prayer request, write it on the bandage and stick it to a metal or hard plastic tray—your "Prayer Platter." As God answers your prayers, let your child move the bandages to the back of the tray.

105

The Prodigal Son

Jesus liked to tell stories. His stories helped people understand what God is like. One day he told this story. You copy what I do, and we'll learn the story together.

Jesus told about a man who had two sons. *(Hold up the index finger of both hands.)* Son number two didn't like working for his father. So he said, "Some day I'll get part of our family's money. I want my part now."

The father felt sad. He knew the boy would take the money and go away. But the father gave the boy the money.

106

Sure enough, the son took the money and went far away to another country. *(Hold up both index fingers again. "Walk" one of the fingers away from the other and put it behind your back.)*

The son couldn't wait to spend the money. He bought fancy clothes. He gave big parties. He had fun with anyone he wanted to, even if some of the people weren't very nice. The son did just what he wanted to do, whether it was right or wrong. He thought he was happier than he had ever been.

But one day the money was all gone. There wasn't a single coin in his money bag. No more parties. No more new clothes. The son didn't even have money to buy food. So he got a job feeding pigs.

The son thought, "I am so hungry. Even my father's servants have clothes to wear and food to eat. I will go home to my father. I will tell him I was wrong for acting the way I did. I will ask to be one of his servants." The son traveled back to his father. *("Walk" the finger that is behind you so that it is in front of you again.)*

When the son was still far away, the father saw him coming. He ran to his son and hugged and kissed him. *(Move your index fingers so that they are next to each other.)*

The son said, "Father, I have done so many wrong things! I'm sorry."

But the father called to his servants, "Bring some new clothes for my son. Make a fancy meal. We're going to have a party! My son, who was lost, has been found!"

Jesus wanted everyone to know that God is like the father in the story. He loves us no matter what. He will forgive us when we ask him. And he is always ready to welcome us into his loving arms.

What a crowd! I can't see anything. If only I were bigger. Aha! There's a nice big tree. And the first branch is low so I can get to it. I love to climb trees, don't you? Up in a tree, I'm bigger than anyone. Here I go...up and up and up. This is much better. I can see. I can see Jesus. And he's coming right toward me!

Jesus knows my name! He wants to come to my house. Jesus wants to be my friend!

I can tell Jesus loves me. He knows I'm sorry for all the wrong things I've done. His love makes my nasty heart feel all clean and warm. Do you know what? I'm going to give back all the money I took. I'll even give back more than I took! Jesus changed my heart! I feel different. I feel good! I'm a new person—all because Jesus loves me.

Jesus loves you too. If your heart feels nasty, tell Jesus you're sorry and he'll fix it. Now I have friends and a happy heart. Thank you, Jesus, for giving me a fresh start!

Honesty

Zacchaeus had trouble making friends because he didn't tell the truth. How do you feel when someone tries to trick you? God wants us to tell the truth and not be sneaky.

Bible Verse

Don't lie to each other
Colossians 3:9

Swoop's Art Cart

Get List: coffee filter or paper towel, bleach, dark food coloring.

Cut a heart shape from a coffee filter or a paper towel. Explain that this heart is like our hearts. Put water and dark food coloring in a container. Explain that when we tell a lie we sin and it puts a spot on our heart. Put little drops of the dark colored water on the paper.

Now explain that when our hearts are full of wrong things we've done, Jesus is like this special water. He can forgive us and make our hearts clean again. Put a drop of bleach on the dark spots and watch them disappear!

Nip & Tuck's Together Time

Make a leaf collection together. The local library will have many books on tree identification. See if you can find a sycamore tree in your town. Try to collect at least 20 leaves from different trees and put them in a book. You might even try having some fun climbing a tree together.

What's in Pouch's Pocket?

Zacchaeus climbed a sycamore tree to see Jesus. A sycamore tree has strong, wide branches that make it good for climbing.

God Talk

Cut out a large letter "T" from construction paper or an index card. Help your child hear the "T" sound at the beginning of the word "truth." Take turns holding the paper "T" as you pray and ask God to help you tell the truth. You can use a response format. The person holding the "T" begins a sentence, and everyone responds: Help me to tell the truth.

When I play with my friends,
Help me to tell the truth.
When I talk to my family,
Help me to tell the truth.
When I do something I know is wrong,
Help me to tell the truth.

The Super-Duper Supper

Every time your child hears a number, ask him or her to clap once. A child who is a good counter can clap the same number of times as the number. An especially alert child may also hear the number sounds within words like "wonderful," "to," "ate," "forgot" and so on. Pause at the words written with a numeral to give your child enough response time.

1 day a boy went on a hike to the Sea of Galilee. The boy carried 1 knapsack with wonderful things inside. He had not forgotten a thing. He had a water jar, a hat, his 3 favorite rocks, a great, big blanket in case it got cold and, of course, 1 supper with 5 barley buns and 2 fish.

The boy traveled with a crowd of people who were following Jesus. Not just 5 people, not just 10 people. More than 100 people. Thousands of people followed Jesus.

The crowd came to a hill. Up, up, up the boy trudged. He did not mind the walk because Jesus was at the top of the hill. The boy forgot how heavy his knapsack was. The nearer he got to Jesus, the faster he walked.

Jesus sat at the top of the hill with his 12 disciples. They saw the crowd coming. Jesus asked a disciple named Philip, "Where can we buy bread for these people to eat?"

Philip answered, "I could work hard for 8 months and not have enough money to buy bread for all these folks. They wouldn't even get 1 bite."

Andrew, another disciple, had a good idea. "Here is 1 boy with a good lunch. He has 5 barley buns and 2 tiny fish. But I don't think it's enough for this crowd."

Everyone sat down on the grass in groups of 50 or so. Next Jesus took the 5 barley buns and 2 tiny fish and prayed over the food. Jesus passed out pieces of tender fish and barley buns. The 5 buns became more than 5,000 buns. The 2 fish became more than 10,000. Jesus gave some food to the boy, too. Everyone ate and ate and ate the great food. When they were done, the 12 disciples picked up the leftovers. There were more pieces than when Jesus started: 12 basketfuls!

1 by 1 the people left and said to each other, "Surely this man is the special 1 sent by God."

Go for the Godprint

Helpfulness

The little boy in the story gave his food to Jesus. Then Jesus did a miracle and made a super supper for everyone. Even though Jesus did most of the work, the boy had a special part in helping. God likes it when we help do his work.

Bible Verse

We will serve the LORD.
Joshua 24:15

Rocket's Rhymes

This simple counting poem has the beat of "One Potato, Two Potato."
One bun *(lift one finger)*
Two buns *(lift two fingers)*
Three buns *(lift three fingers)*
Four *(lift four fingers)*
Five little buns I give to the Lord. *(lift five fingers)*
One fish *(lift one finger)*
Two fish *(lift two fingers)*
That's all—*(lift both hands)*
Pray! *(fold hands in prayer)*
God will meet my needs today.

Bumbles Hops to it

Want a way your family can help spread the Good News of Jesus' love? Buy a loaf of frozen bread dough (or frozen rolls) and bake it with your child. Cover it in plastic wrap and decorate it with ribbon. Give your child an 8 1/2 by 11-inch sheet of paper, folded in half lengthwise. Let your child decorate the top portion of the paper. Fold the paper in half again, widthwise, keeping the decorated part outside. On the inside of the card write this Bible verse: Jesus said, "I am the bread of life. No one who comes to me will ever go hungry" (John 6:35). Along with the verse include an invitation to go to a church function with your family. Give the loaf and card away to a neighborhood family or some friends.

What's in Pouch's Pocket?

The boy in the story was very young, maybe five or so. And his bread was made from barley, which was the kind of grain poor people ate.

God Talk

Go on a short prayer walk in your neighborhood, covering at least four houses. At each house, stop and pray with your child: "Dear God, bless the people in this house. (Use their names if you know them.) If they are in need, show us how to help them. In Jesus' name, amen."

Preciousness

You are precious to God. He made you. He wants you to snuggle up with him and let him take care of you, just like the Good Shepherd takes care of his sheep. Pretend you're a little sheep snuggling up with the Good Shepherd.

Bible Verse

He takes good care of those who trust in him.

Nahum 1:7

Nip & Tuck's Together Time

Good Shepherd Tag—You need one shepherd, one wolf and countless sheep. The wolf is "It." The wolf's job is to turn all the sheep into lamb chops, by tagging the sheep. Once a sheep has been tagged it must freeze into a lamb chop, and you know lamb chops can't move! The Good Shepherd comes to the rescue by tagging the frozen lamb chops, making them into sheep once again. The sheep are free to run and play.

Mouse House Munchies

Get list: Large and minimarshmallows, pretzel sticks, powdered donut holes.

Use a mixture of marshmallows, pretzel sticks and powdered donut holes to create cuddly and yummy little sheep. (The legs are pretzels, body is the donut hole, and the head and ears are a combination of marshmallows.) These delicious goodies can also be used to build a protective little sheep pen. Use the following as a model for some math munchie fun. "If one sheep is in the pen, and two sheep are out of the pen, how many sheep does the Good Shepherd have all together?"

What's in Pouch's Pocket?

The shepherd's job is to find food and water for the sheep during the day. Then he leads them back to a safe place to sleep at night.

God Talk

Make five little sheep using a marker and cotton balls. Find a small basket. Tell your child, **Jesus is the Good Shepherd. He takes good care of us, his sheep. Let's use these sheep to thank Jesus for all the good things he gives us. As we tell Jesus each good thing, we'll put a sheep into this basket to remind us that Jesus, our Good Shepherd, cares for us.**

Jesus' friends cried while he hung on the cross. After a few hours, the sky turned dark, almost black. The sun stopped shining. The earth shook. And Jesus died.

Jesus' family and friends stood nearby and watched. They could hardly believe what was happening. They didn't understand why Jesus had to die. Usually only bad people died on a cross. Jesus wasn't a bad person—he was God's perfect Son.

This was a bad day. But God had a good plan.

Jesus' friends and family felt so sad. They were sad for Jesus, because he died, and they were sad for themselves, because they would miss him.

A friend named Joseph took Jesus' body off the cross. He wrapped Jesus' body in spices and long strips of cloth, then laid it in a tomb. Before Joseph left, he made sure a big heavy stone covered the door to the tomb.

This was a bad day. But God had a good plan. And this isn't the end of the story! Turn two pages to read how Jesus rose from the dead!

God's good plan was for Jesus to take the punishment for the wrong things we do. Jesus loved us enough to do that. Isn't that a good plan?

Unselfishness

God sent Jesus to die on the cross for our sins. He chose Jesus to take the punishment we deserved. Jesus didn't have to do that, but he wanted to help us. It would be like a friend taking your "time out" when you did something wrong. Jesus took our punishment because he loves us. Jesus was unselfish.

Bible Verse

The Son of Man came to look for the lost and save them.
Luke 19:10

Swoop's Art Cart

Get List: two pieces of wood or craft sticks, one shorter than the other; craft glue, string or twine.

The cross is a symbol that children can use to remember that Jesus died for them. Help your child make a simple wooden cross by gluing the sticks together. Help him or her wrap the string or twine around the cross. Let your child be creative on how the twine is draped. Glue the string or twine in place.

This cross can help your child remember that Jesus died for us. Decide together where the cross will be hung. Glue a small loop of string to the back of the cross. When the cross has dried, help your child hang up the cross.

Rocket's Rhymes

Use the following finger play to help your child remember that Jesus died for us.

Jesus died on a cross.
   (Make a cross with the pointer or index finger of each hand.)
He died for you. *(Point to another person.)*
He died for me. *(Point to yourself.)*
Jesus died on a cross.
   (Make a cross with the pointer or index finger of each hand.)
From all our sins *(Cross your arms over your chest.)*
We are set free! *(Open arms wide.)*

What's in Pouch's Pocket?

Usually only people who broke the law were put on a cross to die. Jesus never broke a law and he never did anything bad—he is God's Son.

God Talk

Get List: a piece of scrap lumber, like a section of a two-by-four, a nail with a large head for each family member, a lightweight hammer.

Jesus died for our sins. Let each person pray a short prayer about being sorry for doing something wrong (sinning). After praying, that person hammers a nail into the wood to represent his or her sin. (Be sure to help your children so they don't hit their precious fingers.)

After all the nails have been driven in, close the prayer time:

God, thank you for sending your Son, Jesus, to die for us.

In Jesus' name, amen.

The Butterfly in the Garden

I'm just a little butterfly, but I have a big story to tell. Come closer. I'm very small. I can't talk very loud. Are you close?

Do you see what I see? I know it's dark. But look carefully. Some women are coming to see the place where Jesus was buried. They're going to be surprised. Maybe you know why.

Jesus isn't buried here anymore. Jesus' friends put his body in a cave Friday night. Then they rolled a big stone in front of the hole to the cave. They wanted to make sure no one could get in.

But now it's Sunday. And the stone is not there. I almost got squished when the big stone rolled away. I got out of the way just in time. I've been sitting on that very stone for hours, waiting for somebody to come see the surprise.

The women peeked inside the cave. It was dark and smelly and cold and scary. But they were looking for Jesus. They didn't know where else to look. Surprise! He wasn't there.

How did the stone get moved? Where was Jesus? That's what they wanted to know. They didn't know what to say. They didn't know what to do. Would they ever find Jesus again?

Get ready for the next surprise.

Suddenly there were two angels standing by the stone. They were bright as lightning. Have you ever tried to look at lightning? It's scary, but it goes away in a flash. But the two angels didn't go away. They stayed to talk to the women.

The angels said, "Don't be afraid. Jesus is not here. He's alive! Run and tell your friends."

The women decided to do just what he said. They turned around and ran to tell their friends about the surprise.

What would you do if you saw an angel?

Soon all of Jesus' friends found out that the grave was empty. Jesus was alive!

Jesus was full of surprises. Just when his friends thought they would never see him again, Jesus showed up. He talked to one friend right here in the garden next to the cave. I saw him myself. Then he appeared in a room with a lot of people. Then he cooked breakfast for some friends on the beach.

Some surprises are scary. I get a funny feeling in my tummy. But this surprise was a happy one. It makes my antennae spin and jump, and I can hardly keep my six legs still. How about you?

Jesus is alive!

Joy

Can you think of a word that's even better than happy? How about "joy"? Jesus rose from the dead and lives in heaven to care for us. That's why we celebrate Easter. And that's something to be joyful about all the time!

Bible verse

Always be joyful because you belong to the Lord. I will say it again. Be joyful.
Philippians 4:4

Rocket's Rhymes

Sing to the tune "If You're Happy and You Know It."
Verse 1
If you're joyful and you know it, clap your hands. *(Repeat.)*
If you're joyful and you know it then your face will surely show it.
If you're joyful and you know it, clap your hands.
Verse 2
Jesus Christ has risen. Praise the Lord. *(Clap your hands and repeat.*
Jesus Christ has risen! He has risen from the dead.
Jesus Christ has risen. Praise the Lord. *(Clap your hands.)*

Bumbles Hops to it

As a family, make a basketful of joy to give to an unsuspecting neighbor or friend. Decorate and then fill the basket with items that bring joy, such as, hot chocolate, crayons, stickers, candy, candles and bubbles. Add fun-filled notes and reminders of the reason for the season for extra special touches. Be very sneaky when you deliver the basketful of joy. You want it to be an anonymous surprise.

What's in Pouch's Pocket?

In Bible times, friends and relatives put perfume on the bodies of people who had died. Why? To honor the person who had died and to make things smell better. That's what the women who came to Jesus' grave wanted to do.

God Talk

Shout for joy!
There is so much to be joyful for.
Let's give Jesus a little shout for joy.
Here is a good cheer to show how joyful you are:
Give me a J—Jesus: thank you, Jesus, for dying for me.
(Fold hands together.)
Give me an O—Only: Jesus is God's only Son. *(Hold up one finger.)*
Give me a Y—You: you are precious in his sight.
(Point and cup hands over eyes.)
Jesus gives me Joy, Joy, Joy, Joy, Joy in my heart!
Amen.

Knock, Knock, Where's Peter?

An evil king named Herod didn't want anyone to remember Jesus. He wanted to get rid of all Jesus' friends and stop them from preaching. The evil king killed one of Jesus' friends, then had Peter thrown into prison. Oh, no! God's people didn't want Peter to be killed too. So they started praying.

King Herod knew that sometimes God helped Peter do great miracles. So the king ordered extra guards and put heavy chains on Peter.

"There!" thought the king. "Now it will be impossible for Peter to get out."

But God's people were praying hard for Peter.

Knock, knock,
Who's there?
Guards, lots of guards!

The night was dark and cold. Peter knew that the next day King Herod would call for him. Peter wasn't worried. He knew God's people were praying for him and he trusted God.

While Peter slept between two of his guards, a bright light filled the room. An angel touched Peter

"Wake up!" said the angel. "Hurry and get up!"

As Peter stood up, his chains fell off. He dressed and followed the angel.

Knock, knock,
Who's there?
An angel, bright and strong!

149

The angel led Peter right out of the prison. It seemed impossible. They walked past one guard, two guards, three, four...until they came to the iron gate.

Screech! The gate swung open all by itself. Peter walked out of prison and into the city. He was free! He turned to see the angel, but the angel had disappeared. "Wow!" Peter thought. "At first I thought this was all a dream, but it's real. God sent an angel to set me free from wicked King Herod."

Peter hurried to the house where he knew his friends were praying. He knocked at the door. The servant girl named Rhoda scurried to answer.

Knock, knock,
Who's there?
Rhoda runs to see.

"Who's there?" Rhoda called through the closed door.

"It's me—Peter!"

Rhoda knew that voice. It was Peter. Rhoda was so excited that she forgot to open the door. She ran back and told the others, "It's Peter! He's at the door!"

They thought Rhoda was so excited that she was seeing things. Then the knock came again.

Knock, knock,
Who's there?
It's Peter!

Everyone ran to the door. They heard Peter's voice, threw open the door and welcomed him in. Peter told his friends about the guards and the angel. The friends told Peter how they'd been praying for him. And everyone praised God for this amazing answer to prayer!

from
Acts
18, 24–26;
Romans 16:3–4;
1 Corinthians
16:19

God's People Work Together

Big jobs, little jobs, hard jobs, easy jobs. You try and try and do your best. Sometimes it's nice to have help.

Setting a place at the table for everyone in your family is a big job. Putting all the toys away is a big job. Putting on your own shoes can even be a big job—if you have to do it all by yourself. If someone helps you, the jobs don't seem so big. This is a story about three good friends who worked together to do a big job for God.

Every day Priscilla and Aquila made tents. That was a big job! First they had to tear the fabric—rip, rip, rip. Then they used a needle to sew the fabric together—up and down, up and down. When the tent was all sewn together, they could fold it up and start another one. Maybe they sang a little song while they worked:

(To the tune "London Bridge Is Falling Down.")

Rip, rip, rip, and up and down.
Up and down, up and down.
Rip, rip, rip, and up and down.
Making tents.
Fold it up and start again,
Start again, start again.
Fold it up and start again.
Making tents.

All day long Priscilla and Aquila worked on their tents. Then one day they met a new friend. A man named Paul came to visit them.

Have you ever had a new friend come visit at your house?

Well, Paul didn't just come for a visit. He came to stay. He helped Priscilla and Aquila with their tents. Rip, rip, hurray!

While Priscilla, Aquila and Paul worked on the tents, they talked about Jesus. Paul loved Jesus, and wanted to tell everyone in the world about Jesus' love.

Now that would be a really big job! Do you think Paul could tell everyone about Jesus all by himself?

Priscilla and Aquila wanted to help Paul tell people about Jesus. For a while they traveled around with Paul. They met some people who didn't know about Jesus yet. What do you think they told those people about Jesus?

What would you say to a friend who didn't know anything about Jesus?

In a city called Ephesus, Priscilla and Aquila met a man named Apollos. Apollos knew a little bit about Jesus. Priscilla and Aquila told Apollos more about Jesus. Now Apollos could help them tell even more people about Jesus' love!

Together, Paul, Priscilla, Aquila and Apollos told a lot of people about Jesus' love. Then those people told others. But do you think they told everyone in the whole world?

Telling the whole world about Jesus is a really, really big job! It's a job that all God's people get to do together. If we love Jesus, we get to work together with boys and girls and moms and dads and grandmas and grandpas all over the world to tell people about him. It's a really big job, but with God's help, we can do it!

Go for the Godprint

Community

When Paul first came to Priscilla and Aquila's house, he was a stranger to them. But as they worked on the tents and talked about Jesus together, they became good friends. They liked serving God together! God wants us to serve together too. If you have good friends or people in your family who love Jesus, you can serve God together by telling others about Jesus' love.

Bible Verse

Serve one another in love.
Galatians 5:13

Nip & Tuck's Together Time

Together as a family, volunteer to do a simple service project for your church. Choose a project that your preschooler can help with, such as straightening hymnals after church, organizing canned food for the food closet or washing toys from the nursery. As you work, talk about how your work will help others in your church experience Jesus' love.

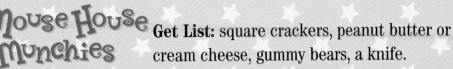

Mouse House Munchies

Get List: square crackers, peanut butter or cream cheese, gummy bears, a knife.

Show children how to make "tents" by leaning two square crackers together, then spreading peanut butter or cream cheese along the top. Give each person three gummy bears to represent Paul, Priscilla and Aquila. As you enjoy the treats, talk about ways you can share Jesus' love at the following places:

- at preschool
- at church
- at the park or playground
- in your family
- in your neighborhood
- with your friends

What's in Pouch's Pocket?

Priscilla and Aquila's church met in their house. What would it be like if your church met in your house?

God Talk

Set up a tent in your living room or yard. (If you don't have a tent, cover a table with a blanket.) Gather your family in the tent. Say a prayer of thanks to God for each family member and friend who loves and serves Jesus.

Pray in your own words, or use the following prayer:

Parent or older child: God, thank you for (name of person).

All family members: (Name of person) loves Jesus.